THE SCARLET THREAD THROUGH THE BIBLE

The Scarlet Thread——
Through
the Bible

W.A.Criswell
PH.D., D.D.

BROADMAN PRESS
NASHVILLE, TENNESSEE

This inspirational book contains the
freely-expressed opinions of its author
and is not to be considered as
a formal statement of Southern
Baptist doctrine.

Dewey Decimal Classification: 234.3
Printed in the United States of America
Library of Congress Catalog Card Number: 70–132923

TO

DR. AND MRS. WILLIAM KENNETH JACKSON,
OUR DEAR DAUGHTER AND SON BY MARRIAGE,
BOTH OF WHOM ARE GOD'S GRACIOUS GIFTS TO US.

FOREWORD

By far, by so far as to be incomparably far, the greatest preaching experience I ever had in my forty-four years as a pastor was upon a day when New Year's Eve fell upon a Sunday night. It came about like this.

Some of my godly deacons said to me: "Pastor, you never have enough time to preach. You never finish your complete sermon. Now, at the end of this year we notice that our annual watch night service comes on a Sunday. Why do you not begin at our usual time at 7:30 o'clock and preach through until midnight? We'll stay with you and in that way you can finish your message." They said this sort of facetiously, for even though I preach forty-five or fifty minutes, I still complain about the brief time I have to present God's Word. The more I thought about their fanciful suggestion, however, the more it appealed to me. Finally I announced that come Sunday night on New Year's Eve I would start preaching at 7:30 and continue until past midnight. If people wanted to come and to listen, they were welcome, but they were to come prepared for the marathon.

When I went to the service and looked out upon the

congregation, I was overwhelmed. We have one of the largest auditoriums in the nation, yet that night it was packed upstairs, downstairs, and with men and women standing around the walls both on the lower floor and in the balconies. But as great as was my surprise at the beginning of the service, I was even more amazed at the termination. After I had preached for several hours and had come to the conclusion past midnight, the lower and upper floors of our auditorium were still packed with people standing around the walls, both downstairs and upstairs. Nothing like that had I ever experienced in my life. The dear Lord was with me in power all the way through.

This sermon is presented in this little volume you now hold in your hand. It was taken off a tape transcription, corrected for better reading (there is such a vast difference between speaking and writing), and is published in the hope and with the prayer that God will bless it to your hearts as He did to the hearts of those who were present on that memorable night.

And, by the way, I still did not have enough time to deliver the completed message! There are literally a thousand things left out that should have been included in the development of the theme. Maybe God will give me a planet, someday, somewhere, beyond this life, when I can preach to my heart's content. Oh, how much there is to be said about Jesus!

God bless you as you share with me this sermon from God's Holy Book.

W. A. CRISWELL

CONTENTS

PART ONE THE CREATION AND THE FALL

We are going to stand, as it were, on a great and lofty eminence and look over the entire story of human history, from its beginning in the unknown distant ages of the ageless past, unto the vast, incomparable consummation of the ages which are yet to come.

Before time was, God the Spirit—God the Almighty Jehovah God—created his infinite, heavenly hosts. He created them in angelic orders. Some of them he called angels, some of them he called seraphim, some of them he called cherubim, and some of them he called archangels. These celestial, spiritual, heavenly beings constituted the first great creation of Almighty God in the timeless ages of eternity past. In that host of God's created, angelic beings, living in the heaven of heavens where God lives, there was the glorious covering cherub, the ruling archangel whom God named Lucifer or "The Son of the Morning."

The second creation which God Jehovah made was this: he created the physical universe. Whenever ministers try to spiritualize religion so as to take the material and the physical out of it, they are getting more religious than God. God likes materiality. He created it. God likes corporality. He created it. God likes these planets and rocks and seas and stars. He likes people. He likes food. He created them. He likes living. He created it. The second great creation of God was this material universe in which we live. The Book opens with Genesis 1:1, "In the beginning"—in the beginning of God's material creativity, producing this world that we see—"In the beginning God created the heavens and the earth." When that beginning was, no one can know. Mind cannot extend itself to enter into it. In the beginning of the beginnings God cast these vast universes out into space and placed them under his unchanging, almighty laws. Everything which God made was beautiful and perfect, filled with light and glory and gladness. His creation of the celestial world was beautiful and perfect. His creation of the material world was beautiful and perfect. Every orb was set in its place according to the celestial ableness of Almighty God. Everything was beautiful.

Then sometime in that beginning, in the ages of the ages past, sometime before time was, there came into the heart of Lucifer, the "Son of the Morning," that marvelous covering cherub in the celestial world, what the Bible calls "sin." We read about him in the prophet Ezekiel. He is described like this: "Thou sealest up the sum, full of wisdom, and perfect in beauty. Thou hast been in Eden the garden of God; every precious stone was thy covering, the sardius, the topaz, and the diamond, the beryl, the onyx, and the jasper, the sapphire, the emerald, and the carbuncle, and gold: the workmanship . . . prepared in thee was perfect and beautiful. Thou art the anointed cherub that covereth; and I [says the Lord God] have set thee so: thou wast upon the holy mountain of God; thou hast walked up and down in the midst of the stones of fire. Thou wast perfect in thy ways from the day that thou wast created, till iniquity was found in thee. . . . therefore I will cast thee out as profane . . . Thine heart was lifted up because of thy beauty, thou hast corrupted thy wisdom by reason of thy brightness: I will cast thee to the ground . . . Thou has defiled thy sanctuaries by the multitude of thine iniquities . . . therefore will I bring forth a fire from the midst of thee, it shall devour thee, and I will bring thee to ashes" (Ezekiel 28:12–18).

Another passage describing Lucifer, the Son of the Morning, is in Isaiah. "How art thou fallen from heaven, O Lucifer, son of the morning! how art thou cut down to the ground . . . For thou hast said in thine heart, I will ascend into heaven, I will exalt my throne above the stars of God: I will sit upon the mount of the congregation . . . I will ascend above the heights of the clouds; I will be like the most high taking God's place. Yet thou shalt be brought down to hell" (Isaiah 14:12–15). Somewhere in the infinite, timeless ages sin was born in this covering cherub, this archangel of the Lord God Almighty, under whose care God had placed the heavenly hosts. When Lucifer fell and when sin was found in him, one-third of the angels of heaven fell also (Revelation 12:4). And in the fall of Lucifer and his angels, God's created, material world fell apart. Sin always destroys. Sin plows under. Sin wrecks. Sin grinds. Somewhere in the timeless ages of the past, after God had created the heavenly hosts, after God had created the heavens and the earth and after sin

13

was found in Lucifer, God's great universe fell to pieces. The planets, the sun, and the stars became chaotic masses of fire, mist, and water, wracked by searing blasts of wind. God's beautiful world fell into emptiness, into void, into formlessness, into ugliness and darkness.

Then, God did a miraculous and marvelous thing. In six days—each day with a morning and an evening—God re-created this planet and this universe, the sun and its planets, and our earth. In six days God recreated it, bringing it out of its formless, empty void, out of its darkness, and out of its mists and watery grave.

(Many fine Christians, many devout scholars of God's Holy Word, would question a Second Creation, a re-Creation, a "gap" between Genesis 1:1 and Genesis 1:2—or other attempt to explain the marvelous things the great Jehovah God did before the stirring events in the first chapter of Genesis. If, out of a scrupulous insistence upon correctness of doctrine, you disagree with me at this point, read "Creation" for my "re-Creation" in these pages—and we will settle it in heaven!)

On the first day God said, "Let the light penetrate the darkness." And God's heavenly, celestial light poured into this earth when it was without form and void, when darkness was upon the face of the deep. As the Spirit of God brooded upon the face of the waters, suddenly the formless mass was filled with light.

Preacher, how do you know all of those things? From the Bible. It says here in Genesis 1:2: "And the earth became *tohu wa bohu*," translated here "without form and void," that is, empty and uninhabitable. I turn to the prophet Isaiah: "For thus saith the Lord that *bara*

14

[created out of nothing] the heavens; God himself that formed the earth and made it; he hath established it, he created it not *tohu* [formless]" (Isaiah 45:18).

God never made this universe formless, void, empty, and dark. God made it beautiful and perfect. His material creation was as perfect as was his celestial universe. But sin destroyed it and plunged God's creation into chaos and formless darkness. Isaiah the prophet says that God did not create it in ugliness. Rather, Satan made it so. Sin did it. Iniquity did it. Transgression did it. Now, after Satan's fall, God is recreating his universe. On the first day he pierced it with the glory of his light. "And God said [by fiat], 'Let there be light.' "

On the second day he created the firmament. He separated the waters above from the waters beneath. On the third day he created the seas. He put the waters together and the dry land appeared. On the fourth day God made the marvel of the sunset. Why a sunset? A sunset is the most extraneous, useless piece of work imaginable. But God loves things that are beautiful and colorful. So on the fourth day God cleared out the darkness and the mist and took away the darkening clouds and made the beautiful sunrise and sunset to open and close the day. The moon and the stars then embellish the night. The sun, moon, and stars had been created in the beginning. This is the re-creation of God, when God takes away the chaotic darkness into which this earth was plunged and makes the phenomena which we call sunrise and sunset with visible moon and stars which shine and glow. Then on the fifth day he created animal life. All of the species of animals which we see living in the earth, God created in a day. Not in a million, thousand, trillion years, but "by fiat" God created them in a single day by his spoken word. And finally, on the sixth day he created the man and his wife. "And God said, Let us make man in our image, after our likeness: and let them have dominion over the fish of the sea, and over the fowl of the air, and over the cattle, and over all the earth, and over every creeping thing that creepeth upon the earth. So God created man in his own image, in the image of God created he him; male and female created he them. And God blessed them, and God said unto them, Be fruitful, and multiply, and replenish the earth, and subdue it: and have dominion over the fish of the sea, and over the fowl of the air, and over every living thing that moveth upon the earth" (Genesis 1:26–28).

Every once in a while I will meet with somebody who looks with great theological askance upon a trip to the moon. But we are to remember that God has given unto man all of his universe, to subdue it and to have dominion over it. If they offer me a trip to the moon and promise me a safe return I'm ready to go. I would like the experience. All of God's creation is to be brought into subjection. The fowls of the air (and we can out-fly them), the fish of the sea (and we can out-swim them), and everything which God has made, he created for man to have dominion over and to rule over. God created man to be as God's son, and under the Almighty, to rule over God's domain.

God then placed the man he had made in the Garden of Eden which was located in the southern part of the Mesopotamian Valley. I know that because of the naming of the rivers which poured through that beautiful Garden. One is named the Euphrates, and another is named *Hiddekil*, or the Tigris River. Those two rivers flowed through the beautiful Garden of Eden. There God began anew and again with his re-created world.

Into this re-created paradise came a sinister being, the serpent. We know him after he was cursed, crawling on his belly, licking up the dust of the ground. But the serpent was at one time the most beautifully adorned and the most gifted of all of the created beings which God had made in this world with the exception of the man. Whatever he looked like and with whatever identities he possessed, the serpent lent himself to Satan. Now Satan is spirit, and a spirit has no body or corporality. Spirits have to get into people if they are to assume bodily form. "Ah," you say, "that's medieval folklore, theological superstition." Listen! I have seen evil spirits enter into the hearts of people—the spirit of lying, the spirit of deception, the spirit of violence, murder, meanness, iniquity. All kinds of spirits enter into the hearts of people. And Satan chose to enter into this most beautiful and gifted of all God's creation outside of the man and his wife. In that serpent, Satan did an astonishing thing. He began to speak in human language to the beautiful woman who was perfect and glorious, fashioned by the hand of God out of the "side" of man.

You have it translated "rib," not "side," in Genesis 2:21, 22. But the only place that word is translated "rib" in the entire Hebrew Old Testament is right here. Everywhere else it is translated "side," as in the "side" of the ark. You would not say the "rib" of the ark, but rather the "side" of the ark, or the "side" of the tabernacle. Out of Adam's "side" God took Eve. Adam looked upon her and said, "This is bone of my bone and flesh of my flesh." And he loved her and took her unto

17

his heart. Satan saw it and began to speak to that beautiful woman.

What is the greatest struggle of the ages? Some may say that the greatest conflict of all time must be the struggle unto death between the freedom of our democracy and the tyranny of ideological totalitarianism. Some could say it was the conflict in the wars which swirled around Germany. Some could say it was the terrible campaigns which wracked Europe under Napoleon. Some could say it was the devastating wars of the Caesars. But through the ages the greatest conflict of all is between the evil of Satan and the mind and love of God. In glory Lucifer looked upon the pre-existent Lord Christ and said in his heart, "I would be first, I would reign, I would rule." He hated Jehovah Jesus, the Lord Christ, in heaven and decided to supplant him and to destroy him.

You see, Heaven loved the Lord Jesus. It is hard to say these things in human speech because he was known by the name of "Jesus" only in his incarnation. But in the beginning of the beginnings, before time, before the ages, there was the uncreated God and the uncreated Christ. When God said, "Let *us* make man," the plural pronoun refers to God the Father, God the Son, and God the Holy Spirit, the triune personality of God into which conception a man's mind cannot enter. Our limited intelligence cannot understand it. We cannot fathom it. But in heaven, in that spiritual world before time was, was the Lord Christ. Satan envied him and hated him and lifted up his soul against him to suppress him. It is against the Lord Christ that Satan in all of his subtlety wages war day and night. Satan chooses to take God's world away from him and has

18

avowed to rule over God's world in the place of the Lord Christ. When God made the universe, Satan said, "I will seize it." When Satan saw the man and the woman in the Garden of Eden, in the perfection and beauty of the Almighty, Satan said: "I will destroy them. I will prohibit them from ruling over the universe under Christ. I am going to seize the power for myself, and I am going to destroy the man; *I* am going to reign and to rule over this creation."

From the beginning all of this was known to the sovereign God. And from the beginning the Lord Jesus came forward and volunteered to be redemption, forgiveness—to be the sin-bearer and Savior of Adam's fallen race. When Jesus met the tempter in the wilderness of Judea, that was just one tiny segment of the conflict between those two: between Lucifer, Son of the Morning, and Jesus the Christ, the Lord God. The story in Matthew 4:1–11 is just a small segment, a small link, in that awesome conflict between Jesus and Satan which started in heaven before the world was. It started before time was, this bitter conflict between the hatred of Lucifer and the love and compassion of the Lord Christ for his creation and for his people.

Thus, in the Garden, in the beginning, the serpent is used by Satan to speak to the woman whom God had made. How does Satan tempt the woman? What does he say to her? He does not have anything new to say. His every approach is old. We know what he is going to say before he begins. There is no new attack on God by Lucifer. We know exactly what he is going to say.

First, he is going to put a question mark after the Word of God. "Yea, did God say that? Did God tell you there is a hell? Did God say to you there is a judgment? Did God say to you if you sin you will die? Did God say that?" First a question mark, and then a lie, the first lie. "You shall not surely die," a denial of God's word. Then Satan presented to Eve the fruit of the tree of the knowledge of good and evil. The woman then ate when she was tried and deceived by the serpent. She thereupon took the fruit to Adam. But Adam was not deceived. Adam knew that the moment he ate he would die. Satan deceived the woman, but he did not deceive the man. When Adam saw Eve partaking of the fruit of the tree of the knowledge of good and evil, Adam made a choice. He so loved her, and he so found his soul bound with her, that Adam chose to die by her side, rather than to live without her. I cannot help but speak words of infinite admiration for the first federal head of our human race. He chose to die with Eve, whom he loved, rather than to live without her. God could have made another Eve. He could have made a half-dozen Eves. But Adam chose to die by the side of that beautiful and gloriously created woman whom the Lord had placed in his arms, close to his heart.

When God came to visit the man and his wife in the cool of the day, he could not find them. He raised his voice, "Adam? Adam? Where art thou, Adam?" Out of the covering of the trees in the garden, Adam answered: "I heard you coming. I was afraid." God said, "Afraid? Who made thee afraid? Who taught you that word 'fear?' Afraid?" Adam said, "I was afraid for I am naked and my wife is naked." The Lord said, "Who taught thee thou wast naked?" Then the story is recounted to the Lord Almighty. When they said in the presence of God that they had made themselves fig leaves to cover their shame and their nakedness, the

Lord looked upon them and said: "But it will not do. Not what human hands can weave. It will not do." And somewhere in the Garden of Eden the Lord took an innocent animal, and before the eyes of Eve and Adam, God slew that innocent animal and the ground drank up its blood. This is the beginning of "The Scarlet Thread Through the Bible." With the sacrifice of an innocent animal, God took coats of skin and covered over the shame and the nakedness of the man and his wife. This is the first sacrifice, and it was offered by the hand of Almighty God. I have often thought that when Adam saw the gasping, spent life of that innocent creature, and when he saw the crimson stain which soiled the ground, it was his first experience to know what it meant to die because of sin. So the story of atonement and sacrifice begins and unfolds throughout the Word of God until finally in glory we shall see great throngs of the saints who have washed their robes and made them white in the blood of the lamb. This is "The Scarlet Thread Through the Bible."

PART TWO THE STRUGGLE BETWEEN EVIL
AND GOOD

In the Garden of Eden, as the Lord covered over the nakedness of the man and the woman, he
turned to Satan and said, "The seed of this woman,
whom you have deceived and through whom you have
destroyed the human race, will crush your head." For
centuries the old rabbis poured over that word of
Jehovah God to Satan. "The seed of the woman." Seed
is masculine; seed belongs to the man. A woman does
not have seed. The old rabbis poured over that word
and the promise of God that the seed of the woman shall
crush Satan's head. The promise is related to the long
conflict and struggle between the hatred of Lucifer
and the love of God in Christ Jesus. It speaks of Jesus
Christ, the seed of the woman, finally defeating Satan
at Calvary. Jesus suffered. His heel was bruised. But
in that bruising, he defeated once and for all the power
of that old serpent, the devil. He crushed his head.

The man and the woman were driven out of the
Garden of Eden, but they were not left without hope.
The Lord placed on the east side of the gate cherubim
and an altar. Wherever in the Bible you find cherubim,

they are always symbols of the grace, love, mercy, and forgiveness of the Lord God. He placed the cherubim there and also the altar for the man to come to in repentance and in faith. Thus a way was provided for the sinful man to draw nigh to God. The Lord guarded the Tree of Life lest the man eat of it and never die. It was a merciful thing for God to do. Had our first parents eaten of the Tree of Life they would have been confirmed in this body of death forever. This would have been the most tragic of all the imaginable things that could have overwhelmed the human family. Death is a release. I do not want to live forever in this body of death with my eyesight gone, my hearing gone, my back stooped, my frame disintegrated. I would dread to be confirmed forever in this body of death never able to die. In his mercy God took away and out of sight the Tree of Life lest the man eat thereof and live forever. "Flesh and blood cannot inherit the kingdom of God; neither doth corruption inherit incorruption" (I Corinthians 15:50). God has made it possible for us to exchange this old house of clay, with its infirmity and its senility, for a house not made with hands, eternal in the heavens (2 Corinthians 5:1). That is why he took away and placed under guard the Tree of Life. Someday, the Book says, we shall find that Tree of Life in glory, in the paradise of heaven.

So God drove out the man and his wife. In the passing of time she bore two sons. One was named Cain, and the other, Abel. Cain brought to that altar east of Eden the first fruits of the field like a displayer at a county fair. He was very proud of himself as he laid it at the feet of God in his pride. Abel, feeling himself unworthy and undone, by faith brought a lamb, the firstling of his flock, and poured out its blood, offering it upon the altar. God respected Abel for the faith in his heart and received his sacrifice. But God respected not Cain because of the pride in his heart. Cain was like Lucifer who lifted himself up and boasted of himself. When Cain saw he was rejected, he lifted up his hand against Abel and slew him. Then was raised the first mound in the earth. Underneath it lay a boy. And Adam and Eve knew what it meant to die in the loss of that boy, Abel, and Eve's tears watered the soil above the grave.

In the goodness of God, the Lord gave Eve another son, Seth. Now Seth was a man of faith, but Cain was driven out from the presence of the Lord as a blasphemer. The Bible story follows the progeny of those two: the line of Cain, the children of the devil; and the line of Seth, the children of God. As long as the children of God were separated, God blessed the earth, the world, and its families. But in the sixth chapter of Genesis a tragic thing came to pass. The sons of God, the children of Seth, looked upon the enticements of the world and lusted after them. They turned from their separateness, their dedication, and their holiness; and they began to marry into the families of the sons of Cain. God looked upon it and saw that his children had forsaken his altars and had turned from their holy vows of consecration. The whole earth was filled with violence and evil and iniquity. Whenever a girl comes to me and says she is going to marry a worthless drunkard she says, "You don't understand, Pastor. I'm going to make a Christian out of him." Do not ever think that when God's people intermarry with the vile and the iniquitous of the world they are going to lift them up to God. Rather, the evil ones are going to pull God's children down to death. That is exactly what happened in the earth as recorded in Genesis 6. The children of God began to marry into the line of Cain, and the fallen progeny filled the earth with violence, blood, murder, and blasphemy. Finally God said: "It is enough. It is enough." He looked over the whole human race, the children of old man Adam, and found that there was only one righteous man in the whole earth, just one. That man's name was Noah.

God said to Noah: "It is enough. It is enough. One hundred and twenty years from now I am going to destroy this world by a flood. Make for yourself an ark and bring your family in." Out of his compassion for the world that he had made, the Lord God told Noah to bring into the ark seven of a kind of the species which were clean and two of a kind of the species which were unclean. So Noah built that great ark after the specifications dictated by the Lord. It was made and fashioned after the finest nautical symmetry known today. Then God shut Noah up in the ark.

When the rain began to fall, and the floods began to rise, and the people beat on the door of that ark, why did not Noah open the door to let them in? Because God had shut that door. There is a day of grace beyond which a man cannot trifle with God. Known to him, there is a time, a line drawn which when a man goes beyond, he will never be saved, never. I suppose you could call that "the unpardonable sin." God shut the door and that race, that generation, was destroyed.

After the water subsided God opened the door, and Noah came out. Here is the beginning of all the nations of the earth described in the tenth and eleventh chapters of the Book of Genesis. The nations of the earth are divided into three parts. The sons of Noah were Shem, Ham, and Japeth. The sons of Japeth became what one would call the Aryans, the Indo-Europeans. The second son, Ham, became the father of the Canaanites, of the Egyptians, of the Africans, of the Philistines. The third, Shem, was the father of the Semites, the Elamites, the Chaldeans, the Assyrians, the Syrians, the Hebrew families, the Arabians.

In that faraway day the people were all one, and they all sought to be together as families do. But God had told them to inhabit the whole earth and to have dominion over the whole creation. When all of those families, therefore, came together in one place as recorded in Genesis 11, they began to build a great, central monument to keep together. They also thought that if there was another flood (which God had promised never would be again) they would have a tower which would reach up to heaven in which they could escape from the water. When God looked down and saw the pride of men in their hearts, He confused their speech and caused them to "babel." Being unable to understand each other, those who spoke one language went in one direction, and those who spoke another language automatically went together in another direction, and those who could speak a third language turned still another direction. So they divided up according to their speech, according to the family tongue, according to the mother language. They separated from Babel and covered the whole face of the earth. Thus nations of the earth grew up from those three great sections of the family of Noah.

PART THREE FROM THE CALL OF ABRAHAM THROUGH THE TIMES OF THE JUDGES

The first eleven chapters of the Book of Genesis concern the whole family of the human race and constitute God's introduction to his Bible. Beginning at chapter twelve in the Book of Genesis there is introduced the one family whom God has chosen and through whom he will keep that promise, "I will give thee a seed that shall crush Satan's head." In the twelfth chapter of Genesis we are introduced to Abram, who lived in Ur of Chaldea at the bottom of the Mesopotamian Valley where the Tigris and Euphrates Rivers flow into the Persian Gulf. To him God said, "Get thee out of thy country, and from thy kindred, and from thy father's house, unto a land that I will shew thee" (Genesis 12:1). Abram lived in an idolatrous city, and his father was an idolater. His father's name was Terah. It is said that he manufactured idols and sold them. God told Abram to get out. God further said to him: "I will make of thee a great nation, and I will bless thee . . . And I will bless them that bless thee, and curse him that curseth thee: and in thee shall all families of the earth be blessed" (Genesis 12:2–3). So out of the family of Shem, God chose Abram from Ur of Chaldea.

But at first Abram did not leave his father's house and father's family. Instead, from Ur of Chaldea he went up to the northern part of the Mesopotamian Valley to a place called Haran. Abram, his brother Nahor, his father Terah, and Lot, his brother's son, all moved up to Haran. There later Abraham sought a wife for Isaac (Rebecca), and there Jacob lived for twenty years as a servant of Laban in return for the hands of Leah and Rachel in marriage. After Terah, the father of Abraham, died, Abraham took his bride, Sarah, and his nephew Lot, and moved down to the promised land. He came to Shechem, then to Bethel, then to Hebron, then to Egypt for a while because of famine, and then back to Hebron. In Hebron he and Lot parted ways, and Lot went down into the cities of the plain where he pitched his tent toward Sodom and later became the mayor of that wicked city.

The angels of the Lord came and said to Abraham, "Because the sin and iniquity of that outrageous city has come up unto God, we shall destroy it." Then the angels left, but Abraham stood yet before the Lord, knowing that Lot was in that city, righteous Lot, vexing his soul with the filthy living of the Sodomites. Abraham prayed to God: "If fifty righteous be found, would you spare it for the sake of fifty? For forty? For thirty? For ten?" Had he asked that the city be spared for the sake of just one righteous man, God would have granted his request. But Abraham went no lower than ten. The angels could not find ten righteous men in Sodom. There, as Lot looked on, and as Abraham looked on from Hebron, the fire fell on Sodom and Gomorrah after Lot, his wife, and two daughters had been snatched away. Jesus says this is a picture of his coming, "Likewise also as it was in the days of Lot" (Luke 17:28). At the end of the age God's people must first be taken out before the fire and brimstone can fall. At Hebron Abraham looked and saw the destruction of the cities of the plains. Then Abraham moved to Beersheba.

In Beersheba follows the story of Isaac and Abraham and later the story of Isaac and Jacob. Isaac's life is first enmeshed with his father Abraham and later with his sons, Jacob and Esau. In Beersheba, mother Rebecca loved Jacob, but father Isaac loved Esau. Jacob is very shrewd and most domesticated. His brother Esau is a fine specimen of an animal. You would have liked Esau. He would have been the captain of the football team. He was a hunter and a fisherman; he loved a hunt with the dogs. He liked the out-of-doors. That is Esau. All the way through, Esau is sensual and carnal. He was of this world. He liked the things of the flesh. Isaac liked Esau because he ate of Esau's venison. Thus it came to pass that, upon a day, when Esau was returning from a hunt and perishing to death from hunger, he sold his birthright to Jacob for a mess of pottage, for some soup. Then with Rebecca, Jacob cheated Esau out of his father's blessing, having already purchased from his brother his birthright. In bitter anger Esau said, "I will kill you." So Jacob fled away to Padan-Aram, up there where Nahor lived in Haran, to the north of the Mesopotamian Valley.

Jacob fled away, but, as he fled, he stopped at Bethel where God confirmed to him the promise of the seed, and of the land, and of the Savior who was to come. From Bethel and its vision of angels Jacob went to

Padan-Aram, to Haran, up there in the house of the grandson of Nahor, whose name is Laban, the brother of Rebecca. He worked for Laban seven years for the hand of Rachel, and then, of all things, when he woke up the following morning and looked at the woman to whom he had been married the night before, she was not Rachel at all. I have always thought that was one of the most astonishing things that a man ever did. Jacob could not tell in the nighttime whether it was Rachel or not. He should have known her better than that. So having married Leah by trickery, he worked seven more years for Rachel. Then he worked six more years for Laban.

At the end of twenty years God told Jacob to go back to Palestine. So Jacob came back from the east side of the Jordan and crossed over to Shechem. Living there in Shechem, Simeon and Levi did a cruel and awful thing in destroying the men of Shechem. Then finally, Jacob came to Bethel, where he renewed his vow to God, and from Bethel he went down to Hebron. While he was on the way to Hebron, Rachel died at Bethlehem.

Down at Hebron, Israel's boy, Joseph, was sent to Dothan, which is about ten miles north of Samaria, in order to find the flocks and his brothers who were keeping them. When Joseph appeared, his brothers said, "There's that boy that our father dotes on and spoils with his coat of many colors." They proposed to slay him, but Reuben persuaded them to spare his life. Thus it came to pass that they sold him to the Ishmaelites. These traders took him down to Egypt. In Egypt Joseph became the prime minister under Pharaoh. In later years there was a famine in the land of Canaan, and the brothers of Joseph went down into Egypt to buy grain.

They came back for their father, and in Egypt, in the time of famine, they were given the land of Goshen to live in. As you look at Egypt it has a triangular delta where the different branches of the Nile River pour out into the Mediterranean Sea. On the right side of the delta, between the delta and the desert, is a little area which is named Goshen. It is very fertile. There Pharoah and Joseph settled Jacob or Israel and his family. Then we read of the death of Joseph and of his extracted promise from his brethren that his bones will be carried back into the promised land when God visits them.

But there arose a Pharaoh that did not know Joseph. Having fled from Pharaoh to the back side of the desert, at Sinai Moses was tending sheep. While he was caring for the sheep at the foot of Mount Sinai, God spoke to Moses out of a burning bush. God said: "I have heard the cry of my people. I am sending you to deliver them." Moses said, "Anybody but me, anybody but me." But the Lord answered: "No, it is you. My people, through whom this promise is to be made and kept inviolate, must be delivered." Moses went down to see Pharaoh after the ten plagues. It was a night of nights. On that night of nights, they took a lamb and slew it, poured out its blood, and sprinkled that blood with hyssop (a common, ordinary, mistletoe type of a bush) on the lintel and on the doorposts on either side in the form of the cross. "When the death angel passes over tonight," God said, "when I see the blood I will spare you and your home." But in all the other homes and families there was death, wailing, and lamentation throughout Egypt, all except to those who were under the blood. "The Scarlet Thread Through the Bible."

That night Israel went out with a high hand; they

crossed over the Red Sea by the providence of God; turned down south until, in the third month of the exodus, they stood there at the base of Mount Sinai. On Mount Sinai for forty days and forty night, Moses was with God. The Lord gave to Moses first the moral law (Exodus, chapters nineteen and twenty). Then God gaves Moses the civil law (Exodus, chapters twenty-one to twenty-four). Then God gave to Moses the ceremonial law (Exodus, chapters twenty-five to forty) with its tabernacle, its priesthood, and its sacrifices.

In the Book of Leviticus we have in chapters one to seven the sacrifices described. There are five of them: the burnt offering, the meal offering, the peace offering (or the thanksgiving offering), the sin offering, and the trespass offering. The difference between the sin offering and the trespass offering is one of volition. The sin offering is for a wrong done volitionally, while a trespass offering is for an inadvertent sin which a man did not mean to do. Those five sacrifices are given in the first seven chapters of the Book of Leviticus. In chapters eight to ten is the consecration of priests; in chapters eleven through fifteen, ceremonial holiness; in chapter sixteen, the Day of Atonement; in chapters seventeen to twenty-three, all of the festivals; and in chapters twenty-four to twenty-seven, the vows, tithes, and laws of obedience. Every convocation of Israel is a happy one, a feast, except one. That is the Day of Atonement. The Jews observe it until today, calling it Yom Kippur. A Jew may not act like a Jew any other time of the year, but on that Day of Atonement, if he is a Jew, he becomes traditionally repentant and devout. The Day of Atonement is described in the sixteenth chapter of the Book of Leviticus.

The Book of Numbers, from chapters one to ten, records the events at Sinai: there is a census taken; there is a consecration of Levites; there is the altar dedication; and there is the observance of the Passover. The second part of the Book of Numbers finds Israel on their wandering march through the wilderness (chapters eleven to twenty-one). They make the journey from Sinai to Kadesh-barnea. At Kadesh-barnea they sent spies into the land in order to see how to conquer it. But instead of coming back with faith and dedication, the spies came back saying that there are giants over there and walled cities. "And we were just like grasshoppers in their sight. We can't conquer that land." However, Caleb and Joshua said: "But God is with us! Let us arise and inherit it for God. He has promised it to us." "No," said those other ten, and all Israel wept and turned back from Kadesh-barnea. For thirty-eight years they wandered in the wilderness. Then they made their way to the plains of Moab. There, on the east side of Jordan, we find the death of Aaron; the story of the fiery serpents; the deceit of Sihon, the king of the Amonites; and Og, the king of Bashan. All of the territory on the east side of the Jordan was given to Rueben, to Gad, and to the half tribe of Manasseh.

On the plains of Moab occurs the story of Balaam and the sin of Baal-Peor. Balaam was hired in order to curse Israel. But God would not let him curse Israel. Now Balaam had to do something to deserve his hire to the king of Moab. He whispered something in the ear of the king of Moab, Balak's ear, and, brother, did it work! Do you know what he whispered in his ear? He said, "You get all the pretty women in Moab together and take them over there and put them near that camp and let's see what happens." Dear me, it really happened! It is unbelievable what pretty women can do, and they did it. After this debacle we follow the story of the final preparation for Canaan.

The Book of Deuteronomy is made up of five great addresses of Moses. The first address is on the history of the forty years of wandering (chapters one to four). The second address is on the law (chapters five to twenty-six). The third address is on the blessings and the cursings (chapters twenty-seven and twenty-eight). The fourth address is on the second covenant (chapters twenty-nine and thirty). The fifth address is Moses' song and his last words. Deuteronomy is a Latin word meaning "the second giving of the law." So after Moses had sung his song, and after he had delivered his soul of these five addresses, then God said to him, "Get thee up into the top of Pisgah" (Deuteronomy 3:27). Moses went up to the top of Pisgah, called Mount Nebo. And the Lord said to him, "Look, this is the land, this is the land." All through the Bible you will find "the land," and "the people," and "the seed" (the Savior Christ), and "the kingdom." "This is the land which I sware unto Abraham, unto Isaac, and unto Jacob, saying, I will give it unto thy seed: I have caused thee to see it with thine eyes, but thou shalt not go over thither" (Deuteronomy 34:4). So Moses the servant of God died there in the land of Moab on Mount Nebo, and God buried him in a valley. No man knows of his sepulchre until this day.

After the death of Moses, God said to Joshua, "Moses my servant is dead; now therefore arise, go over this Jordan, thou, and all this people, unto the land which I do give to them, even to the children of Israel"

(Joshua 1:2). Is not that amazing? God says he gives it to them, but they have to fight for it with their lives. They are contested for every inch, just as God says to us today, "Go, make disciples," but it's hard. "Go, preach the gospel," but it is difficult. "Go, make every man conscious of the love of Jesus, preach to him." Ah, Lord, but that is a hard assignment. But that does not matter. God has those whom he will give us. Whenever a man preaches the gospel, somebody will be saved. When a man builds a church, God will add to it. Not all will be saved before Jesus comes again, for there will always be people here who will reject, but there will also always be people here who will respond, whatever the difficulty, whatever the discouragement, whatever the trials. "Go over," God says, "there are victories for you." The Lord will give us somebody.

Thus Joshua went over Jordan and began the wars of the conquest. He made three campaigns. First, in the center of the country, he took Jericho. It was in Jericho that the incident happened which gave rise to the title of this message. The scouts sent out by Joshua to spy out Jericho were saved by the faith and the kindness of Rahab. The men of Israel promised her life and safety, both for her and her father's house, if she would bind a scarlet thread in her window. This she faithfully did, and, when Jericho was delivered into the hands of Joshua by the mighty intervention of God, Rahab and her family were spared because of that scarlet line. "The Scarlet Thread Through the Bible."

After the conquest of Jericho, Joshua took Ai, which was the military outpost and bastion of Bethel. Then Israel was deceived by the Gibeonites with whom they made a truce in compromise. So Israel won all of the central part of the country. Then Adonizedec, who was the king of Jebus, later Jerusalem, with four other kings, warred against Joshua. They were about to win the southern campaign, but, when Joshua prayed for the sun and moon over Ajalon not to go down, there was a long day that resulted in a mighty triumph for Israel. Then up in the north, above Galilee, Joshua fought against Jabin, the king of Hazor, and won the third great campaign. Then the conquest ceased. The last part of Joshua is the story of his death and of his appeal to the people to be true to the Lord.

Now we come to the Book of the Judges. The difference between a judge and a king is this: a king gives to his son in succession his throne, but a judge is raised up according to a crisis and endowed with special gifts from God for that one period of time. First, in the days of the Judges, the hordes out of Mesopotamia, between the Tigris and the Euphrates Valleys, came and oppressed Israel. Othniel, who was the younger brother of Caleb, was the judge raised up to deliver them. Then the Moabites oppressed Israel, and God raised up Ehud to deliver Israel. The king of Moab was named Eglon and the Book says he was very, very fat. Ehud was left-handed. When you are afraid of a man, you watch his right hand. You do not think about his left hand. Upon a day Ehud came to Moab's capital to bear the tribute to Eglon. He laid the tribute down with his right hand, but he had his left hand back of him. When Ehud put the tribute down with his right hand and the big, fat king looked at it in greed and avaricious gladness, then Ehud, who was left-handed, whirled around with his left hand, which had a dagger in it, and plunged the dagger into Eglon. The fat of Eglon covered over the dagger to the hilt, and Ehud could not pull it out. So he just left it in him and fled to safety.

Next is an invasion from Philistia from which Shamgar delivered Israel with an oxbow. Then you have the great invasion from the north under another Jabin from Hazor. Sisera was the captain of the host. There was not a man in Israel who would fight him, not one. All of them were scared to death. So God raised up a woman. Thank the Lord for Deborah. God raised up Deborah who encouraged Barak. They defeated Sisera and the host of Jabin in the valley of Esdraelon. Then you have the Midianites and the story of Gideon. Then you have the Ammonite oppression and Jepthah. And last of all, you have the Philistine oppression and the story of Samson, which brings us to the ministry of Samuel and to the reign of Saul, of David, and of the kings of Israel and Judah.

PART FOUR From the First of the Prophets to the Founding of the Kingdom

The last of the judges was Samuel. Samuel marked the beginning of the emphasis upon a new development in Israel. There is only one religion in the world which is characterized by the phenomenon of prophecy. Only the biblical religion produced true prophets. No other world religion produced men who foretold the future with accuracy, speaking of things which God would do in times to come. Samuel, the last of the judges, is also the first of the prophets. In his life, Samuel instituted what you call a seminary, a school of prophets. And from Samuel on the prophetic ministry more and more comes to the forefront in the life and development of God's people.

The ministry of Samuel is introduced in chapters one to seven. The reign of Saul is described in chapters eight through thirty-one. Samuel, as you know, was born in answer to the prayers of a godly woman named Hannah, a wife who heretofore had been unable to bear children. In answer to her prayer, God placed in her arms this little boy whom she called "Asked of God," or "Samuel." When she weaned him, after three years, she brought him to the house of the Lord at Shiloh, to the high priest named Eli. There, before Eli, the little lad Samuel ministered unto the Lord, being a Levite, dressed in a linen ephod, the plain white garment of a priest.

Samuel grew up before the Lord. Even in childhood the word of the Lord came to Samuel, and no message that he delivered did God let fall to the ground. During Samuel's ministry, he went around with a Bible in his hand and taught the people the Word of God. He made his circuit year after year, teaching people the law of Moses. In Samuel's age the people said to him: "We want to be like the nations around us. We want a king." And God said to Samuel: "Give them a king. Even though the request comes out of rebellious hearts, listen to their vain desires." God had willed, even in the Book of Deuteronomy, that they have a king. But not for the reason the people gave. Anyway, the Lord said to Samuel, "You go ahead and obey their cry." So Samuel chose a godly, handsome, humble, marvelous young fellow by the name of Saul. Is not it a shame that he could not have continued that way? Samuel chose Saul, the son of Kish, and after the anointing of Saul, he was presented to the people. So humble was Saul, so self-effacing, that, when they gathered to crown the new king, he was not even there. They found him hidden away in the baggage. When they brought him out, he stood head and shoulders taller than any of the other men of Israel. They shouted, "God save the king." Is not that a marvelous thing? They still say that word over in England, "God save the king." Thus they crowned Saul.

In his beginning ministry, Saul was a great man and a powerful influence for God. For example, Saul's greatness may be seen when the Ammonites came from the east. The Ammonites were a kind of Bedouin nomadic group, living at the head of the Arabian desert. The Ammonites came and said to the men of Jabesh-gilead: "Come out. We are going to put out your right eyes, every man among you, just to show our contempt for Jehovah God and for you." The men of Jabesh-gilead sent word to Saul that the Ammonites had come and were going to put out their right eyes just to show the Ammonite's contempt for Jehovah God and for God's people. When the new king heard this, the spirit of the Lord came upon Saul. He slew his oxen, cut them up into pieces and passed the pieces around Israel saying: "Whosoever cometh not forth after Saul and after Samuel, so shall it be done unto his oxen. And the fear of the Lord fell on the people, and they came out with one consent" (1 Samuel 11:7). It was a day of revival. It was a day of commitment. It was a day of victory and triumph. Saul led his army across Jordan, routed the Ammonites, and delivered the Jabesh-gileadites who never forgot it. (Read 1 Samuel 31:11-13.)

A series of successful military campaigns crowned the work of Saul. His wonderful boy, Jonathan, attacked the Philistine garrison at Geber and at Michmash. Then he fought the Moabites, the Edomites, and the Syrians. In every way God blessed Saul. But then something happened. I have never understood it. Instead of being that self-effacing, wonderful, humble man who was filled with the spirit of God, he turned into something else. He lost the power of conquest he possessed at the beginning. When he went to fight against the Amalekites, he looked at the treasures of the enemy. He looked at their herds and their flocks, and greed seized him. Every once in a while you see a man like that. A fine man succeeds in the business world, but his success ruins his life. Saul looked at all of the store of the Amalekites, and he desired them. So out of the pride of his life, he thought he would chain King Agag to his chariot and roar back through Judea and through Israel with the king tied to his chariot. He further thought to keep the thousands of sheep and cattle for a gigantic, victorious display. But God had told Saul to destroy everything belonging to the Amalekites. "It is better to obey than to sacrifice," said the Lord God. In his vanity, Saul had begun to disobey God.

In the second Philistine campaign an overwhelming enemy challenger openly portrayed the soul disintegration of Saul. There came out a towering giant by the name of Goliath. All Israel cowered and trembled.

In those days there was a boy, a boy whom Saul did not know. No one thought of him. Even his own father did not call that boy to the feast when Samuel came to the house of Jesse in order to anoint a new king. Here stood Eliab, here stood Shammar, here stood Abinadab, all mighty sons of Jesse. When he had gone through all seven of those boys Samuel said: "I don't understand. God sent me here to your house to anoint a new king, and you say these are all your boys. But God has rejected every one of them because God does not look on a man's countenance; God looks at a man's soul. He looks at a man's heart. I don't understand. I can't understand it." Then the father happened to remember: "Wait. I have another boy." When the boy came, he was ruddy, red-headed, of a fair countenance, but the glory of the goodness of God was in his eyes and on his face. When Samuel looked on him, God said to his prophet: "Arise, anoint him! That is he. This is my new king." A ruddy-faced, red-headed lad from the sheep-fold, yet Samuel anointed him. What an amazing thing!

The next time that lad David appeared, he was sixteen years old. He is growing up to be a young man. We see him walking down the hills to the dry wadi in the middle of the valley called Elah. He walked down into that valley and picked out five smooth, round stones. Did he lack faith that he picked out five stones? If he believed in God surely one stone would have been enough. Why did he pick out five stones? The answer is, Goliath had four brothers. There was one for Goliath and one for each one of the other brothers. He put those five stones in the leather pouch in which he carried his lunch and walked up on the other side of the vale to that glowering giant Goliath, nine feet six inches tall! What a center on a basketball team he would make! There Goliath stood with his spear like a weaver's beam, with his armor-bearer carrying his shield before him, a shield which was higher than a man's head. The giant looked down on that ruddy-faced, slender boy who was equipped with nothing but a shepherd's staff in one hand and something else in his right hand, coming out to fight. Goliath was insulted. At first he did not even get up. He sat down and looked at David and said: "Is this come to me? I'll feed you to the birds of the air and to the beasts of the field." Goliath then stood up and started toward that boy. I presume he was going to seize him by the nape of the neck and manually pull him apart. It was then that the boy reached down into the leather pouch, took out one of those stones, and walked toward the giant, slinging the stone around his head. When he got close, David let go the swirling stone which in turn found its mark. It went straight into the middle of Goliath's forehead and sank into his brain. Goliath fell down dead. David, the boy, took out Goliath's tremendous sword, stood on the top of the corpse, and hacked off his head. It was an unprecedented victory.

When the women of Israel came back to Jerusalem singing about that victory and praising God for the deliverance, this is what they were singing, "Saul hath slain his thousands, but David hath slain his tens of thousands." All the women all of their lives loved David. David must have been one of the most handsome, one of the finest looking, one of the most personable, and one of the best specimens of mankind that the Lord ever created. God loved David. The women loved David. The men who were with David loved him. One time when he was at war with the Philistines, David happened to say, "Oh, I remember the well at the gate of Bethlehem out of which I drank when I was a boy." He just happened to say that, and some of his big, strong, mighty men jeopardized their lives to go beyond the enemy lines to get a drink of water for David from that well. They loved him so. You cannot say too much about David, a man after God's own heart. The women loved him, and Saul heard it. The Book says that from that moment on Saul began to "eye" David. He began to hate him and to seek for his life. Finally David fled the country and was assigned a city in the south of Philistia named Ziklag, there to remain throughout the rest of the Philistine war.

The Book of First Samuel closes with the battle of that third Philistine war. Saul is oppressed as the Philistines gather by the thousands. They are like the sands of the sea, spread out on the plain of Esdraelon (Megiddo). Their very numbers strike terror to his heart. Saul stands with his army and with his sons, Jonathan, Abinidab, and Melchishua, on the heights of Mount Gilboa. In his turn Saul went over on the other side of the valley to a tall hill which looks like a loaf of bread. It is called the Hill of Moreh, and on that hill is a village called Endor. In Endor was a witch, and in the dead of the night, Saul found his way to the witch of Endor and said, "Find me Samuel." Now no witch is able to bring up the dead. No spiritualist, no anybody can bring up the dead. But God let that old hag, that old witch, bring Samuel up because it was for God's purpose. When that witch saw Samuel rise from the dead, her hair stood straight up. It scared the living daylights out of her. She knew she was nothing but a hoax. What happened scared her to death. Saul said to Samuel: "I am oppressed, and the Philistines are gathered like the sands of the sea, and God doesn't answer me any more. I pray, but he doesn't answer. I inquire, and he doesn't answer. God has forsaken me. What shall I do?" Samuel said, "There is not anything you can do when God has left you. Not anything. When God has left you, you are already defeated. By this time tomorrow you and your sons will be with me."

People often ask if Saul was a lost man. No, Sir. Saul was not a lost man. Saul was the kind of a man who lost his ministry; he lost the great ableness of his life. (Read what Paul says of his ministry in 1 Corinthians 9:27.) But he was saved, for Samuel said, "Tomorrow at this time you will be *with me*, you and your sons." Jonathan was one of the flowers of Israel, and wherever Jonathan was going, Saul was going, and wher-

44

ever Samuel was, Jonathan and Saul were going to be. Saul is the type of a man who is called of God and who is endowed with great talents from God. But, instead of using those talents for the Lord, success turned his head, and Saul lost his kingdom, lost his children, and lost the great open door which God had set before him.

The next day Saul joined the battle. The Philistines came up the side of the mount, and Israel rushed down to face them. In that day the Philistines slew Jonathan. He was the first to fall. Then they slew Abinidab. Then they slew Melchishua. Then they began to strike toward the terrorized Saul. When Saul saw that he was going to perish, he took his sword, put the butt end of it on the ground and the point of it in his abdomen, and he fell with all of his great weight on that avenging sword. He lay there in a pool of blood. When the Philistines found him they cut off his head, took off his armor, and fastened his body to the wall of Bethshean, a Canaanite city at the bottom of Jezreel. They took his armor into the house of their goddess, Ashtaroth. When Saul's friends of former years, the men of Jabesh-gilead, heard about it they went at night and took down the body of Saul and buried him at Jabesh-gilead, on the other side of the Jordan River.

Second Samuel marks the reign of David. Chapter one to four speak of his reign in Hebron. Chapters five to eleven deal with his reign over all Israel until his great sin. Chapters twelve to twenty speak of the penalty for his sin, and chapter twenty-four concludes the life and ministry of David. As Second Samuel begins, an Amalekite comes running up to David saying: "I slew Saul, I slew him. Here is his crown, and here is his bracelet." He thought he would be rewarded. David had refused for years to take advantage of the iniquity of Saul and God's rejection of him. David had waited upon the Lord. So incensed was David that he took that Amalekite and slew him. Then David composed a beautiful eulogy honoring Jonathan and Saul. It was at this time that David left Ziklag and was crowned king over Judah at Hebron. David was crowned three times: first, privately by Samuel at Bethlehem; then by the tribe of Judah at Hebron; and finally by all the tribes over all of Israel.

After the death of Saul, Ishbosheth, Saul's son, was placed on the throne by Abner, the captain of the hosts

46

of Israel. David reigned only over Judah, the southern part of the kingdom. When Joab, the captain of David's hosts, became afraid that Abner would take his place in a united kingdom, he privately slew Abner. It was one of the most dastardly deeds that anybody ever did. Two defecting and evil soldiers in the army of Ishbosheth then slew their master, and David became king over all of Israel.

The first part of David's life as king of Israel was magnificent. God gave him every victory. He was never defeated. On and on David rose in glory and in power as he extended the empire. Then, in the prime of his life, at the very height of his glory, instead of marching out to meet the hosts of the enemy as a king ought to do, David went soft. He stayed at home and let Joab lead the armies. While he was at home one evening, on a couch on top of his palace, which was built on the hilltop in old Mount Zion, David looked down in the city and saw a beautiful woman. He did not even know her name. That is not love. He did not know whether she was married or not. That is not love. That is lust! That is downright unadulterated carnality. David, to whom God had given the world, David the king lusted after that beautiful woman. He asked who she was, and he sent for her. Later she sent word to him: "I am with child. What shall I do, for Uriah my husband is with Joab fighting against Rabbath-ammon." Then David said: "This will I do." He got himself a pencil and wrote a note to Joab which said: "You have a man in your army named Uriah. He is a soldier from Jerusalem." (You see David had tried to get him to come home and live with his wife, but Uriah said: "The armies of Israel are fighting for God, and I am not staying at home." When he was forced to return to Jerusalem, he sat out in the street and would not go into his house because the armies of God were at war against Rabbath-ammon. David got him drunk, but he still would not go in.) So David wrote that note to Joab and said: "Joab, you press the battle up there next to the wall. When you get right up there next to the wall with Uriah in the forefront, the rest of you fall back and leave Uriah by himself for the Ammonites to slay." That is what David wrote in that note. Then David added: "When the report is made of what you have done, I won't castigate you for your strategy. I will understand!" Joab did that. He took his army and pressed against the walls of Rabbath-ammon with Uriah at the front. Then, in the midst of the battle, Joab gave a secret command, and all the rest of the soldiers withdrew and left Uriah standing there, God's soldier fighting God's battle. The Ammonites slew him, and he died at the hands of the infidels. Joab wrote back to David and said: "The battle is proceeding as planned. We went up, and we withdrew. Uriah, the Hittite, is dead." But the next sentence in God's Book says: "But what David did displeased God."

The next day Nathan, God's prophet, came in and said to David: "Sir, there is in this kingdom a man who has vast flocks. Across the way there is a poor man who has one little lamb, and he nurtures the lamb. The only pet and the only love he has is that one little lamb. That rich man, with great, extensive flocks and herds, had a visitor. Instead of taking from his own flocks, he went across and tore from that man his little lamb and dressed it." David was angry and said: "That scoundrel! He will restore fourfold." Nathan looked at him, pointed his finger and said: "David, thou art that man." Four-fold. And the sword never left his house. Fourfold.

First, the lad born to Bathsheba died. Fourfold. Second, that beautiful son, Amnon, looked upon Tamar, the full sister of Absalom, and he forced her. Absalom kept the bitter anger in his heart, and, after two years, he slew Amnon. Fourfold. Third, Absalom was the most beautiful prince the world ever saw—with his flowing, golden hair, with his marvelous, scintillating presence and personality. All Israel loved him so much they chose him to be their king instead of David. The people rebelled against David, and David had to flee for his life. All Israel loved Absalom the beautiful prince and son of the great king. On the other side of the Jordan River there was a battle fought. When Joab saw Absalom caught in an oak by that beautiful hair, he took three darts and thrust him through again and again. Fourfold. David cried with a broken heart, "O Absalom, my son, my son Absalom, would God I died for thee, O Absalom, my son, my son." Fourfold. Fourth, Adonijah was like Absalom, beautiful, personable, and gifted. When he sought to subvert the kingdom of Solomon, Solomon had him slain. Fourfold. The sword never left David's house. Throughout the Bible, the story of the kings of Judah is bathed in the blood of an avenging sword.

Second Samuel closes with the tragic story of a pestilence in Israel, a punishment for David's sin in numbering Israel. God said to David: "Choose. Shall it be seven years famine? Shall it be three months before your enemies? Or shall it be three days of pestilence?" What a choice! Seven years famine, three months to be pursued by enemies, or three days of pestilence! David replied: "Three days of pestilence. I cast myself on the mercies of God. Maybe God will relent in the severity of his punishment." Thousands and thousands of God's poor people began to die. When David arose one morning he saw the avenging angel with a sword raised over the city of Jerusalem to destroy it. David in his anguish cried to the Lord God and said: "O God, O God, against me and against my father's house let the sword fall. But, O God, spare those innocent people." The Lord said: "Get thee up to Mount Moriah." We have heard of that mountain before. That is where Abraham offered up Isaac. "Get thee up to Araunah's threshing floor on the top of Mount Moriah. Go build an altar, offer a sacrifice." "The Scarlet Thread Through the Bible." "When I see the blood I will pass over you. I will spare the city." David went up and Araunah saw him coming. "I have come," said David, "to build an altar to God and to sacrifice lest the people be destroyed." Araunah replied: "My lord and king, I give you the place. I give you the instruments. I give you the oxen for the sacrifice." "Nay," said David, "I shall buy it. I will not offer unto God that which costs me nothing." So he bought the threshing floor and built the altar. When God saw the blood, he forgave and saved. There they built the temple of Solomon, and there they erected the great altar, and there the prayers and intercession of the children of Israel arose unto the Lord for years and years. Someday, when they rebuild that temple, the songs and praises of God will go up again from that same sacred place.

The first eleven chapters of First Kings describe the reign of Solomon. The second part of First Kings, chapter twelve to twenty-two, give the story of the divided kingdom to the days of Ahab, king of Israel, and Jehoshaphat, king of Judah.

The account is instructive.

Apparently what we have seen in the reigns of Saul and of David is a pattern of life. Solomon begins gloriously, as did Saul and as did David. God loved Solomon, the Book says, and crowned him with every gift. At Gibeon God said, "Anything, Solomon, you ask shall be yours." Solomon asked for wisdom in order to rule his people well. God said, "Because you have asked for that, I'll give you everything else; I'll give you fame; I'll give you fortune; I'll give you an extended kingdom. If you will be faithful to me I will give you length of days." (1 Kings 3:14.) Solomon began gloriously and triumphantly. The Lord extended his kingdom and blessed him on every hand. But then, Solomon fell into the most tragic decline of any king whose life story one could follow. God said, "You shall not multiply unto you gold and silver." But Solomon did just that until gold was as common in Jerusalem as stones on the street. God had said a second thing. "You shall not multiply unto you wives." God hates that thing. But Solomon multiplied seven hundred wives and three hundred concubines. Think of those concubines! The little Sunday School boy said, "Solomon sure did like women and animals." The teacher said, "What do you mean?" "Well," he said, "he had seven hundred wives and three hundred porcupines!" The closing ministry of Solomon is tragic indeed. His empire fell into disorder, and Solomon died in abject failure.

Upon Solomon's death Rehoboam was made king. A life of lightness and frivolity and foolishness describes Rehoboam. The kingdom divided with Jeroboam to the north, king over the ten tribes of the north, and the line of David enmeshed in the south.

Second Kings is divided like this. From chapters one to seventeen it is a history of the two kingdoms to the fall of Samaria. The last part of the book, chapters eighteen to twenty-five, is the history of Judah to the fall of Jerusalem.

The prophets now are beginning to prophesy; this is the message they bring. There is coming the destruction of Israel, and they prophesy of a terrible scourge from the north.

"The rod of mine anger and the staff of mine indignation." That does not mean that Assyria was any better than Samaria, and it does not mean that Soviet Russia or China is any better than the United States. It just means that God raises up these empires to chasten his people. That is why we tremble today in the presence of Soviet Russia and China. It is not that God favors them or loves them more than us (the favor and blessing of God are upon his people), but if God's people do not get right, and if they do not draw nigh, and if they do not serve God, the Lord raises up bitter, merciless, and cruel nations in order to chasten his people. That is what the prophets were preaching to Israel, "If you do not get right, judgment will inevitably come."

The vast Assyrian hordes came down and carried away the northern ten tribes in 722 B.C. and left Judah alone. Down in Judah the succession of kings continued with Uzziah, Jotham, Ahaz and then Hezekiah. The terrible Assyrian invasion came in the days of Hezekiah. Sargon finally took Samaria and his son, Sennacherib, came down to take Judah. How do you fight a war? With armies and battalions, that is how you fight a war.

Thus thought the Assyrian general. Sennacherib absolutely surrounded Jerusalem and took all of Judah. Hezekiah the king, who was a godly man, made it a matter of prayer. While he was down on his knees talking to God, the voice of the Lord came to Isaiah, the son of Amos, saying, "You go tell Hezekiah that I'm going to put a ring in Sennacherib's nose and send him back by the way that he came. This is my battle, this is my war," says the Lord God. The next morning there were 185,000 corpses when the angel of the Lord got through with the armies of Sennacherib. All this happened in answer to good King Hezekiah's prayer.

After King Hezekiah there follows the history of Judah until finally we come to the last great revival under Josiah. They repaired the house of the Lord and, on the inside of the house of the Lord there was found the Bible which had been lost in the rubble. Whenever people read the Bible you will have a revival.

But during that marvelous turning to God a disastrous thing happened. Pharaoh-Necho, who was the king of Egypt, made an agreement with the remnant of the Assyrian hosts from Nineveh, the capital city which had been destroyed exactly as Nahum had prophesied. Pharaoh-Necho was going to join hands with the Assyrians in order to stop forever the rise of those Babylonians under Nabopolassar and his son, Nebuchadnezzar. When Pharaoh-Necho took his army to Megiddo, on the plain of Esdraelon, to join the armies of Assyria to fight against Nabopolassar and his son, Nebuchadnezzar, Josiah, good King Josiah, who had sworn allegiance to Babylon, took his little army and, there on the plains of Megiddo, tried to stop Pharaoh-Necho in his onward march to the north. What Pharaoh-Necho did was what you would think he would do. He ran over the little army of Judah and slew Josiah, the good king.

Pharaoh-Necho joined the Assyrians at the head of the Mesopotamian Valley in a little place called Carchemish, and at Carchemish was fought one of the great battles of all time. Nebuchadnezzar, who was one of the ablest generals and one of the greatest kings who ever lived, was in charge of the armies of his father, Nabopolassar. There, in 605 B.C., the armies of Nebuchadnezzar overwhelmed the armies of Assyria and of Egypt. So completely were they destroyed that Assyria sank from sight forever and Egypt never rose again as a great power. There, striding across the civilized world, stood that great colossus of a man, Nebuchadnezzar.

In those days Jeremiah lifted up his voice and preached to Judah saying, "Repent ye, repent ye, get right with God." Judah never repented and Nebuchadnezzar came in 605 B.C. from the battle of Carchemish and seized Jerusalem. He look Daniel and the fairest of the royal family to his capital city, Babylon, as captives. Jeremiah lifted up his voice and said, "Repent, repent, get right with God." They never repented, they never got right with God, and Nebuchadnezzar came back the second time in 598 B.C. and took Ezekiel and ten thousand of the fairest into captivity in Babylon. Jeremiah lifted up his voice once again and cried, saying: "Repent, O repent, get right with God. Turn ye, turn ye." They did not repent. They never got right with God. Nebuchadnezzar came the third time in 587 B.C. and did not have to come back anymore, for he destroyed Solomon's temple and beat down the walls of the city and plowed under the holy city of God and sowed it down with salt. He took the people into captivity into the land of Babylon and the whole face of God's earth turned dark and seared, bathed in tears and in sorrow. "By the rivers of Babylon, there we sat down, yea, we wept, when we remembered Zion. We hanged our harps upon the willows in the midst thereof. For there they that carried us away captive required of us a song; and they that wasted us required of us mirth saying, Sing us one of the songs of Zion. How shall we sing the Lord's song in a strange land? If I forget thee, O Jerusalem, let my right hand forget her cunning. If I do not remember thee, let my tongue cleave to the roof of my mouth; if I prefer not Jerusalem above my chief joy" (Psalm 137:1–5). Israel wept and cried and got right with God.

Out of that Babylonian captivity came three great establishments by which God has blessed our world. One, the Jews were never idolatrous again. No Jew has been an idolater since that time. Second, the synagogue was born. And from the synagogue came the church. The services of Judah are the same kind of services we have today. Third, out of the captivity came the canon of the Holy Scriptures. The old rabbis began to pore over the books and to read the prophets and to teach the people the Word of God. It was in keeping with Israel's devotion to the Bible that Jesus came with the scroll of the prophets in his hands, saying, "This day is the scripture fulfilled in your ears" (Luke 4:21). O the wonder of the blessing of God as he guides through human history to that ultimate and final consummation! Out of tears and suffering come our greatest blessings. "The Scarlet Thread Through the Bible."

PART SIX

FROM THE PROPHETS TO THE CHRIST
TO THE PREACHING OF PAUL

In 587 B.C. the Southern Kingdom was destroyed and Nebuchadnezzar, one of the ablest, one of the mightiest, one of the most capable, one of the most unusually endowed of all the kings of all history, who is mentioned more times in the Bible than any other heathen king, carried away into Babylon all of those who lived in the country of Judah and in the city of Jerusalem. Jeremiah was forced by the remnant to go into Egypt and there he died. The prophet Jeremiah had predicted that after seventy years the people of the captivity would have opportunity to return.

Nebuchadnezzar was not only a great general; but he was also a mighty builder. He made Babylon one of the most beautiful cities of the world. But Nebuchadnezzar had a tremendous weakness. He never trained anybody to succeed him. So the kingdom of Nebuchadnezzar disintegrated quickly after his death.

In 538 B.C. Cyrus the Persian took Babylon from Belshazzar without a battle. It just fell into his hands. Daniel, as you know, describes that fall in the fifth chapter of his book. In a night Cyrus took the city of

Babylon while King Belzhazzar and his noblemen were in a drunken orgy. King Cyrus, who founded the Medo-Persian empire, is named as one of God's anointed men. In Isaiah 44:28 and in Isaiah 45:1, hundreds of years before Cyrus was born, the prophet called him by name and spoke of his divine mission. The decree went out from Cyrus that the Jew would have opportunity to go back to his homeland in Palestine, to rebuild his city in Jerusalem, and to rebuild his temple.

The first six chapters of the book of Ezra describe the return of Zerubbabel to Jerusalem with about forty thousand Jews to rebuild the Temple. The second half of the book, chapters seven through ten, describe the return of the priest, Ezra, who came to purify their worship. The ten chapters cover a period of about eighty years, from 536 to 457 B.C. In the midst of the ministry of Ezra, Nehemiah came back to Palestine and to Jerusalem to rebuild the wall of the city. In those final days the last prophets of Israel arose to deliver God's message, Haggai, Zechariah, and Malachi.

The first and the oldest of the writing prophets is Joel. He flourished about 825 B.C. From about 800 to 750 B.C. there were three prophets, and they happen to be the only three who prophesied in the northern kingdom. They are Jonah, Amos and Hosea. About 700 B.C. there prophesied under Uzziah, Jotham, Ahaz, and Hezekiah, the prophets Isaiah and Micah. Then from about 650 to 600 B.C. there prophesied Zephaniah, Nahum, Obadiah, and Habukkuk. In Babylon, contemporary with Jeremiah, God raised up Daniel and Ezekiel. While Jeremiah was preaching in Jerusalem, Daniel and Ezekiel were delivering God's message in Babylon. Finally, there are three prophets of the restoration.

Haggai apparently was an old, old man who had seen the destruction of the temple at Jerusalem, who had been taken into exile, and who had returned back to Palestine with Zerubbabel and Ezra. He was encouraging the people to rebuild the temple. The optimism of Haggai, the old, old man is wonderful to behold. When Haggai looked at the rubble, the debris, and the impossible assignment of those few ragged Judeans to rebuild the temple and the city and the kingdom, he must have beheld one of the most hopeless projects in the world. But Haggai, that old, old man who had seen Solomon's temple destroyed, who had lived through the entire captivity, and who had gone back with Zerubbabel, cried aloud saying, "God says that this second Temple you build will be more glorious than the Temple of Solomon." How could it be? Because the Lord Jesus was to walk into that second Temple built under Zerubbabel.

Of the three great restoration prophets, Zechariah is far and away the greatest. Zechariah spoke so much about Israel, the end of time, and the conversion of the people of the Lord. Then the last prophet, of course, is Malachi. Malachi preached about 450 to 425 B.C. He closed his prophecy with the coming of the Lord: "And the Lord, whom ye seek, shall suddenly come to his temple, even the messenger of the covenant, whom ye delight in: behold, he shall come, saith the Lord of hosts. But who may abide the day of his coming? and who shall stand when he appeareth? for he is like a refiner's fire" (Malachi 3:2–3). In the last chapter, Malachi prophesies, "Behold, I will send you Elijah the prophet before the coming of the great and dreadful day of the Lord" (Malachi 4:5).

The interbiblical period marks the rise of the Hellenistic empire. Alexander the Great, who was a pupil of Aristotle, had a passion for Hellenizing the world as Paul had a passion for Christianizing it. God used the great Hellenistic empire to spread abroad one culture and one language which made possible the preaching of the gospel of Christ to the civilized world. When Paul wrote the letter to Rome, which was the capital of the Latin World, he wrote the letter in Greek. Wherever a man lived in the days of the Roman Empire, if he could read, he read Greek. If he was educated, he knew Greek. The circumference of the Mediterranean world knew the Greek language, Greek customs, Greek culture, and Greek philosophy, art, science, and literature. Alexander covered the whole world with his Hellenizing, missionary work.

When Alexander the Great died, the kingdom broke into four parts. Casandra took Greece, Lysimachus took Asia Minor, Seleucus, whose father was Antiochus, took Syria, and Ptolemy took Egypt. In the first part of the inter-Biblical period, Palestine was under the Ptolemies and it was very quiet. The high priest ruled. But in 198 B.C. Antiochus III overwhelmed the Ptolemies, and Palestine passed into the hands of the Seleucidi (the Seleucids), and the little country was plunged into perpetual turmoil. The Syrian kings were extremely cruel. One of them, Antiochus Epiphanes, seized the temple and offered a sow on the altar in the Temple court before the sanctuary. He took the juice of that sow and poured it all over the sanctuary to defile it. He then dedicated the holy temple to Jupiter Olympus, to Zeus, the Greek name of the god. He interdicted circumcision. He interdicted the observance of the sabbath. He interdicted the Jews' entire religion. Upon a day in the little town of

Modin, located about seventeen miles northwest of Jerusalem, a cowardly Jew was about to bow down and to worship at an altar of Jupiter Olympus. When he did, an aged priest nearby by the name of Mattathias looked upon it. Mattathias lifted up his arm and slew that cowardly Jew. He then bared his arm again and slew the emissary from Antiochus Epiphanes who was demanding the worship of the Hellenistic, heathen god. Then this man, aged priest Mattathias, fled with his sons into the mountains where they carried on guerrilla warfare against the Syrians.

The first son of that aged priest Mattathias to carry the banner of Jewish worship was named Judas Maccabeus, or Judas the Hammer. Judas Maccabeus lead his guerrilla revolutionaries (to the amazement of the world and to the astonishment of any student of history) to complete military success. He won Jewish independence from Antiochus Epiphanes. When Judas lost his life, Jonathan, his younger brother, carried on. When Jonathan was killed, Simon carried on. Simon the Maccabean founded the Asmonaean, or Maccabean, dynasty. His son was John Hyrcanus whose son was Alexander Jannaeus. Alexander's wife was Alexandra Salome, and her two boys were John Hyrcanus II and Aristobulus II. They were feuding among themselves in a civil war over who would reign and rule over Judah when the Romans came. Pompey arrived in Palestine in A.D. 63 with his Roman legionnaires and, after listening to the quarrel between John Hyrcanus II and Aristobulus II, just took the region himself and made it a part of the Roman Empire.

The Jews who were in sympathy with Hellenism were called Sadducees, and those who were very much opposed to Hellenism were called Pharisees. When Jesus came upon the scene, he immediately was confronted with these two antagonistic parties. The Pharisees were very strenuously devoted to the law and against any kind of pagan, foreign intervention. On the other hand, the Sadducees lived to do business with Rome or with anybody who would provide them the emoluments of their office and keep them as rulers and leaders among the people. In those days Herod the Great, an appointee of Rome, was king of the Jews.

When Augustus Caesar was the Roman emperor, and when Rome had the entire world in her hand, the great prophecy of Isaiah, and the great prophecy of Micah, and the great prophecy of Jacob to his son Judah, and the great promise of God Almighty to Eve the woman, came to pass. In the seed of the woman and in the seed of Abraham shall all the families of the earth be blessed—and our Savior is born into the world. "The Scarlet Thread Through the Bible." Why does he come? Albert Schweitzer in his famous theological book entitled, *The Quest For The Historical Jesus*, puts forth the thesis that Jesus Christ came into this world expecting the apocalyptic, messianic kingdom of heaven to come down. When the expected kingdom did not apocalyptically come down, Schweitzer says that Jesus died in disappointment, in despair, of a broken heart— dejected, outcast, disowned, denied. But to us who believe the Bible and preach the Word of God, it is the exact and diametrical opposite. Our Lord came into this world to die for us sinners. That is why he came, according to the Word of God. His death is not one of those cheap burlesques; nor is it a divine comedy; nor is it like one of those Greek tragedies where a nemesis

61

follows some one who is to be destroyed. Rather, the death of Christ was planned from before the foundation of the world, when he gave himself at the beginning to be the redemptive means of God for the purchase to himself of Adam's lost and sinful race. This theme is "The Scarlet Thread Through the Bible." He came into the world to die. "And thou shalt call his name Jesus: for he shall save his people from their sins" (Matthew 1:21).

As Jesus began his ministry, he did so under the shadow of the cross. Through the man sent from God whose name was John, the Almighty introduced his Son, "Behold the Lamb of God" (John 1:19 and 36). Think what that meant to any Jew, "Behold the Lamb of God." Every morning and every evening for centuries the people had witnessed a sacrifice with the blood poured out and the lamb offered unto God for the sin of the nation, for the expiation of all of the iniquity of the people. "Behold," said John the great Forerunner, "behold, the Lamb of God that taketh away the sin of the world."

In his ministry, Jesus early began to teach his disciples that he should suffer and die. When he was transfigured, there appeared Moses and Elijah talking to him about his death which he should accomplish in Jerusalem. When he was anointed by Mary of Bethany, he said it was for his burial. When the Greeks came to see him from afar he said, "And I, if I be lifted up from the earth, will draw all men unto me" (John 12:32). At the last supper he said, "This is my body; eat in remembrance of me." And again he said, "This is my blood; drink in remembrance of me." Before he went to the cross, he gave himself in Gethsemane in travail of soul for our redemption (Isaiah 53:11). And when he bowed his head and died he said, "It is finished" (John 19:30). When we preach the cross, when we preach the blood, when we preach the sacrificial death of Christ, we are preaching the meaning of his coming into the world. The sacrifice of Christ consummated the great redemptive plan and purpose of God in the earth. This is the scarlet thread through the ages.

On the third day our Lord was raised from the dead and appeared first to Mary Magdalene. Then he appeared to the rest of the women. Then he appeared to the two disciples on the way to Emmaus. Then he appeared to Peter alone. Then, that night, that Sunday night, he appeared to the ten disciples, Thomas being absent. Then next Sunday night he appeared to the disciples, all eleven of them. That is one reason I like to have church on Sunday night. The Lord met with his disciples at night and revealed himself to his disciples at night. Later, he revealed himself to the seven at the Sea of Galilee. Then Jesus appeared to over five hundred at one time on an appointed mountain in Galilee. Then after counseling with his disciples in Jerusalem, he ascended up to heaven from the top of Mount Olivet.

It was upon that occasion, at his ascension, that the disciples asked, "Lord, wilt thou at this time restore again the kingdom of Israel?" (Acts 1:6). There is a kingdom coming. God has not failed in his purpose. But in the meantime, until the kingdom comes, the Lord has introduced a great intermission, a great interlude, a great parenthesis. That is the *musterion* or "mystery" in the third chapter of Ephesians, which the apostle Paul says the prophets did not see and the Old Testament never refers to or mentions. There is to be a parenthesis between the time of the rejection of the King and the Kingdom and the time when the King and the Kingdom shall come from God out of heaven. In this period of time which we call the age of grace, the age of the church, Jew and Gentile, male and female, bond and free, all are invited to belong to the household of faith in Jesus Christ. The Lord said to his disciples, "You are to be witnesses of these things." He did not say, "You are to bring in the Kingdom." He will bring in the Kingdom. There will be sin and rejection, and violence here. Daniel said, "Wars are determined unto the end" (Daniel 9:26 ARV). Until the great war at Armageddon men will be dividing up and preparing for war. They will be in conflict. We shall never bring in the Kingdom, but we are to be witnesses of the great salvation and we are to offer it to the world of lost men. We all are invited in the love and grace of Jesus to belong to the glorious household of faith. "Come, come, come!" We are to be witnesses of the grace of God until that great and final denouement at the end of the age. In this way and with this message the first Christian disciples began to preach.

First, the gospel was preached by Peter to the Jews only in Jerusalem. Then, second, the gospel was preached by Philip, a Hellenist, to the half-Jew, down in Samaria. Then, third, the gospel was preached to a Temple proselyte, a full Jewish proselyte, to the Ethiopian eunuch on the road to Gaza. Then, next, the gospel was preached to a proselyte of the gate, to a Gentile centurion in Caesarea. Then, in the eleventh chapter of the Book of Acts, the gospel was preached to out-and-out idolaters, to heathen Greek worshippers in Antioch. These converts came directly out of their idolatry into

64

the glorious faith of the Son of God. Finally, the Lord said, "Separate me Paul and Barnabas to the work whereunto I have called them." And Paul went out to proclaim the gospel message to the whole wide pagan world.

Thus the gospel began to expand over the then-known earth. First Peter, the apostle to the circumcision, offered the gospel to the Jew. Then the Lord raised up Stephen as a bridge bewteen Peter, the apostle to the Jews, and Paul, the apostle to the Gentiles. Stephen, a Hellenist, pointed out that God cannot be contained in a temple made out of stone. Stephen showed that Abraham worshipped God in mountain tops, and that Moses worshipped God on the back side of a desert. Stephen was the bridge between Simon Peter's preaching to the Jew and the apostle Paul's preaching to the Gentile. Paul proclaimed that a man can be saved without ever having anything to do with the Jewish religion. A man does not have to keep the ceremonial law. He does not have to be circumcised. He does not have to keep the Mosaic commandments. All a man has to do to be saved is to turn, to repent, to give his heart and love to Jesus, and God will save him forever. "If thou shalt confess with thy mouth the Lord Jesus, and shalt believe in thine heart that God hath raised him from the dead, thou shalt be saved. For with the heart man believeth unto righteousness; and with the mouth confession is made unto salvation" (Romans 10:9, 10). "For whosoever shall call upon the name of the Lord shall be saved" (Romans 10:13). That is the gospel of Paul.

Paul preached this gospel on his first missionary journey. He went from Antioch down to Seleucia, the port city. Then he crossed over the sea to Cyprus, began his ministry at Salamis, and finally came to the Cyprian capital city of Paphos. Paul then journeyed one hundred and seventy miles across the sea to Perga in Pamphilia, then turned inland to Pisidian Antioch, and from there went down to Iconium and Lystra, and finally arrived at Derbe. Retracing his steps, he went back to Attalia on the sea and thus returned to Syrian Antioch. But when he arrived in Antioch, he had trouble on his hands because the other apostles were not preaching that a man could be a Christian just by trusting Jesus. This deep difference gave rise to the famous Jerusalem conference recorded in Acts 15. The Judaizers argued that a man must be circumcised before he could be saved. They avowed that a man must keep the law of Moses before he could become a Christian. "A man can't be saved just by trusting in Jesus," they said. "He must be circumcised," they added. "No," said Paul, "a man is saved by faith and not by works. He is saved just by trusting Jesus." They had that notable conference at Jerusalem in which the Holy Spirit vindicated exactly what Paul was preaching. The Gentile Christians were free from the unbearable yoke of the law.

Paul went back to Antioch and began his second missionary journey. With a chosen companion from Jerusalem named Silas, he retraced his steps to all the churches which he had already organized in Galatia. Then the Holy Spirit sent him down to Troas. He did not know where to go from there for he had come to the end of the road at the sea. That night Paul saw a Macedonian in a vision who pled, "Come over into Macedonia and help us." Thereupon he crossed the Hellespont into Europe. He went to Neapolis, to Philippi, to Apollonia, to Amphipolis, to Thessalonica, to Berea, and finally to Athens and to Corinth. Crossing over the sea to Ephesus and to Caesarea, he went up to Jerusalem and back to Antioch to end the second great missionary journey.

After the passing of time, Paul began his third missionary journey. He went by land again, retracing his steps in Asia Minor, and came to Ephesus where he had his greatest results. The whole province of Asia was turned upside down, or rather rightside up, in his marvelous ministry at Ephesus. All Asia heard the word of God. After persecution broke out against him at Ephesus, the apostle went to Macedonia and Corinth again, then back around through Macedonia down to Miletus, and finally back to Jerusalem where he was arrested.

When Paul was taken into custody by the Roman soldiers in Jerusalem, for two years he was kept in prison in Caesarea. At the end of two years, having preached to Felix, Festus and to Herod Agrippa II, Paul was taken by Julius, the centurion, to Rome. There in Rome for two years, in his own hired house, he preached the gospel of the Son of God, no man forbidding him. That was about A.D. 63. About A.D. 64 he was liberated and through the few years that remained until A.D. 67 he was at liberty to declare the good news in Christ Jesus. Paul was with Timothy at Ephesus. He left Timothy in the Asian capital while he went up to Macedonia where he wrote First Timothy. He was with Titus in Crete, and, leaving him there, he went up to Nicopolis on the western side of Greece where he wrote the letter to Titus. Then, about A.D. 67 Paul was arrested again. Just before Nero died, Paul was beheaded on the Ostian road down the Tiber from the city of Rome to the sea.

He closed his life with a triumphant word, "I have fought a good fight, I have finished my course, I have kept the faith: Henceforth there is laid up for me a crown of righteousness, which the Lord, the righteous judge, shall give me at that day: and not to me only, but unto all them also that love his appearing" (Second Timothy 4:7, 8).

The epistles of Paul are divided into four distinct groups. The first group he wrote on his second missionary journey from Athens and Corinth. They are First and Second Thessalonians. The second group of letters were born in his third missionary journey. While he was in Ephesus, he wrote First Corinthians. Somewhere between Ephesus and Corinth, he wrote Second Corinthians in Macedonia. Then, either in Antioch or on his way to Antioch, he worte Galatians and Romans. First and Second Corinthians, Galatians, and Romans, therefore, center around the city of Ephesus. The third group of epistles Paul wrote from the prison in Rome, during his first Roman imprisonment. They are Philippians, Philemon, Colossians, and Ephesians. The fourth and last group of his epistles, which were written after his first Roman imprisonment, were First Timothy, Titus, and Second Timothy, called the pastoral epistles.

Each one of Paul's epistles has to do with a very definite subject. The first group (First and Second Thessalonians) has to do with the second coming of our Lord. Paul had preached the gospel and had delivered his soul of the great hope which we have in Jesus. Some of the people had died, and the Lord had not come. What about our beloved dead? Will they share in the Kingdom when it comes? Will they live again to see the face of Jesus, even though they have died and the Lord has not come? Paul wrote First and Second Thessalonians to answer these questions about the coming of the Lord. The next group of epistles (First and Second Corinthians, Galatians, and Romans) has to do with the great Pauline theme that "the just shall live by faith." We are saved by trusting in Jesus and not by the works of the law. That is the great central theme of the second group of Paul's letters. The third group of letters (Philippians, Philemon, Colossians, and Ephesians), has to do along with other things, with the Gnostic philosophy which tried to discount the deity and glory and person of Jesus. Then, of course, the fourth group of epistles (First Timothy, Titus, and Second Timothy), has to do with the ordinances of the church, the doctrines of the church, the offices of the church, and with other practical ecclesiastical matters.

We come now to the conclusion of the
Bible. John alone of the original apostles is left alive. All
of the other apostles are dead, all of them. The apostle
Paul was slain, just before Nero's death, either in the fall
of A.D. 67 or in the spring of A.D. 68. Simon Peter was
crucified upside down just about the same time, in the
eastern part of the empire. All of the other disciples
have been dead for thirty or forty years. Only one of
them is alive, and that is the aged pastor of the church
at Ephesus, beloved John. The Lord had said to his
disciples, "When you see the legions standing at the
gates of Jerusalem, flee." (Compare Luke 21:20–24.)
So they fled to Pella on the other side of the Jordan.
About A.D. 69 John, the aged disciple whom Jesus
loved, came to Ephesus. In that Asian capital God gave
to him his greatest ministry. There he wrote his gospel,
there he wrote his three epistles. But God gave to John
also another marvelous thing. In exile, under Domitian,
God gave him the privilege of writing down the Apocalypse of Jesus Christ (the Revelation). The Apocalypse is the unveiling of the Lord Jesus Christ in his

glory, in his majesty, and in his kingdom. "Thy kingdom come," we pray, and it is surely, surely coming. The Apocalypse, the unveiling of our Lord, is the reward of God to Jesus for giving his life for the sin of old man Adam. It is the unfolding of God's exaltation of his Son for this victory over Satan and the power of death. Because Christ has done this for us, God has also highly exalted him and given him a name which is above every name, that at the name of Jesus every knee should bow, and every tongue should confess that Jesus is Lord to the glory of God our Father. The unveiling, the Apocalypse, the uncovering of Jesus Christ in his glory, in his majesty, and in his kingdom, is the reward that God gave to Jesus for saving us, Adam's fallen children, from our sins.

On the Isle of Patmos, a rocky little point in the sea several miles southwest from Ephesus, John was exiled to die of exposure and starvation. But even there does the Lord appear to John in an incomparable and glorious vision. He heard a voice as of a trumpet and, when he turned to hear and to see, he looked upon his risen and glorified Lord whom he last saw as he ascended into heaven. But this time, oh, how triumphant and how marvelous! The face of the Lord was like the shining of the sun, and his feet as if they burned in a furnace. His majestic robes were girded with a golden girdle, and his hair was white like the snow. His eyes were like a flame of fire, and his countenance was like the sun shining in his strength. When John saw him, he fell at his feet as one dead. The very life was taken out of him. In the old familiar way (for *His* heart never changes; he is still the same Lord Jesus) the exalted Christ placed his right hand on the shoulder of his beloved and sainted disciple and said: "Do not be afraid. There is nothing to fear. Do not fear death, do not fear the grave, do not fear the judgment, do not fear eternity. I am he that was dead and am alive forevermore, and I have the keys of the grave and of death. *I* have them. Do not be afraid." After commanding the apostle to write down what he saw, the Lord gave him the three-fold outline of the Apocalypse: "Write the things which you have seen, and write the things which are, and write the things which shall be hereafter."

In obedience John took up his pen and began to write. He first wrote the things he had seen, the vision of the glorified Lord, walking in the midst of the seven golden lampstands, Jesus among his churches. Then, second, he wrote the things that are, the things concerning his churches. Here they are: here is a church, there is a church, yonder is a church, just as it was in the days of John. The things that are: his church at Ephesus, his church at Smyrna, the one up there at Pergamos, the one at Thyatira, the one at Sardis, the one at Philadelphia, and the one at Laodicea, seven of them as typical of them all through the centuries. Then third, write the things which shall be, *meta tauta*, "after these things," after the churches are no more.

Thus in prophecy (for the Revelation is a book of prophecy) John wrote down "the things which are"; namely, a preview of all God's churches to the end of the age. There is an Ephesian period in the church, a Smyrnan period in the church, a Pergamean period, a Thyatiran, a Sardian, a Philadelphian, and a Laodicean period in the church.

The Ephesian period of the church was that apostolic era closest to the days of the Lord. The Smyrnan period was that period which extended over the days of the Roman Empire. It was a church of martyrdom and suffering. The Pergamean period witnessed the tragic time when the church was married to the world. The Thyatiran period of the church depicts an era when the church in her riches is likened unto an adultress with the world (Revelation 2:22), a church further described in the Revelation, chapter seventeen. The Sardian period of the church is the church of the great Reformation when only a few names are standing out for God (Revelation 3:4). Balthasar Hubmaier and Felix Mantz, John Calvin, Martin Luther, John Knox —a few in Sardis who walk with the Lord.

The Philadelphian period of the church is the period of the open door (Revelation 3:8). That is the reason why I think we are coming to the close of the Philadelphian era. The doors are beginning to shut. You cannot preach the gospel in China. You cannot preach the gospel in Cuba. You cannot preach the gospel in Soviet Russia. You cannot preach the gospel in eastern Europe. The doors are beginning to close on Philadelphia, the church of the open door. We are nearing the close of the Philadelphian age, and we are approaching the beginning of the last age. This is the Laodicean period of the church, when the church comes to its final consummation in the earth. Those in the Laodicean church are at ease in Zion, with the world on fire. They do not care. With the world facing its great climactic day, they are not praying, they are not evangelizing, they have ceased to be burdened for the lost.

In the fourth chapter of the Revelation, under the symbolism of the rapture of John unto heaven (Revelation 4:1, 2), the church is taken out of the earth, and it does not appear anymore until the coming of the Lord in the nineteenth chapter of the book. With the church raptured away, in the meantime down here on this earth there arrives the day of the Lord, the Great Tribulation spoken of by Joel, by Zechariah, by Jesus, and by the apostles. The great final, consummating, judging day of the Lord finally comes.

That awesome time is introduced with the rapture of the church. The Lord comes (between the third and the fourth chapters of the Revelation) secretly, clandestinely, furtively, like a thief in the night. He is coming to steal away his jewels, his pearl of price, the souls for whom he gave his life and did die. He is coming for us, the redeemed of the Lord. He is coming without announcement. There is no sign, there is no token, there is no harbinger, there is no warning, there is no anything. Any moment, any day, any hour, any time, our Lord can come. There is no prophecy remaining to be fulfilled. There never has been anything between the imminence of the appearing of our Lord and his coming for us. Nothing! He may come any day, any time.

It may be at midday, it may be at twilight,
It may be, perchance, that the blackness of midnight
Will burst into light in the blaze of His glory
When Jesus comes for His own.

O joy, O delight, should we go without dying,
No sickness, no sadness no dread and no crying.
Caught up through the clouds with our Lord into glory,
When Jesus comes for his own.

H. L. TURNER

When he comes for us, our beloved and sainted dead are resurrected first, then those of us who remain are caught up to be with them and our Lord in the air (1 Thessalonians 4:13–18). That is the first thing. We go away to be with our Lord, and there, before the judgment seat of Christ (the *Bema*), we receive our reward for the deeds done in the flesh. Our judgment for sin is already pronounced at the cross. Our judgment before Jesus at the end of time is to receive the rewards of our lives. That is why you cannot receive your reward when you die. Your life still lives on. Paul is still living, even in the Book out of which I preach. These old infidels, such as Voltaire and Tom Paine, are still living also. Every once in a while you will run across a young fellow reading Tom Paine or Voltaire and ready to curse God in the language of Paine and Voltaire. These great blasphemers are also living on. You do not die when you leave this earth. You cannot get your reward when you die. The reward is given at the end time. Our lives go on and on and on, and only God can unravel the skein and follow the strand until it reaches its consummation at the end. When the Lord comes, we and the sainted dead shall be changed in a moment, in the twinkling of an eye, at the last trump (1 Corinthians 15:52). When all of us are taken to be with the Lord, then we shall go with our Savior into glory and there stand before him to receive our crown for what we have done in his Kingdom work. With our rewards bestowed upon us, we shall enter with our Savior to share with him the marriage supper of the Lamb.

While God's people are with their Savior in glory, this tragic world down here will enter a dark tribulation. In the turmoil and terror of the nations, there will arise a man who will present himself as the great deliverer of the earth. He says he will bring peace, victory, glory, and triumph. Oh, what he promises! To Israel, going back to their homeland, he promises their land, their nation, their temple, and their people. He promises everything. But he is the anti-Christ. For three and one-half years the world and all Israel follow him. Then, in the middle of that seven-year period of tribulation, he turns into a fiend. At that time will come the most tragic and awesome wave of world anti-Semitism this earth has ever known (Daniel 9:27).

That anti-Christ, the beast who rises out of the sea, has by his side another beast, a false prophet, who is arrayed in all of the glory and splendor of the ecclesiastical systems. That false prophet makes a covenant with that beast, the ruler of the world, the great dictator of the end time. With this support, the anti-Christ, the beast, presents himself as the triumphant leader of all the nations of the world to lead them to peace and to glory. But, in the midst of the seven year period, the beast breaks that covenant with Israel, and the earth is plunged into terror, bloodshed, and horror. But God reaches down in his mercy and seals twelve thousand out of Judah, and he seals twelve thousand out of Simeon, and he seals twelve thousand out of each of the twelves tribes of Israel. God knows exactly where each one of those Judeans or Simeons or Reubenites or Gadites is. In the days of that awful and tragic trial, God is going to seal twelve thousand out of each one of those tribes. The sealing will be their conversion to Christ. These one hundred forty-four thousand are going to preach the gospel of the Son of God. In the midst of that blood, furor, and horror, there is going to be the greatest revival the world has ever known. The converts to Christ are going to suffer unbelievable persecution and martyrdom. But in death they will be welcomed into heaven. As Revelation 7:14 avows, "These are they who are coming out of the Great Tribulation, who have washed their robes and made them white in the blood of the Lamb." "The Scarlet Thread Through the Bible." It began in Eden, it ends in glory.

In the Apocalypse there now follows the seven seals and the judgments thereof, the seven trumpets and the judgments thereof, the seven vials and the judgments thereof, and the seven personages and the judgments thereof. There are the beast (the anti-Christ), the false prophet (the woman in scarlet), and the world-systems, all moving toward the great judgment day of the Almighty. The anti-Christ who professes to be the leader of the nations of the world, is gathering the armies of the entire earth together. They are converging from the north in Russia, from the east in China, from the south in Africa, and from the west in Europe and the islands of the sea. They are converging for that great day of the Lord. That is the Battle of Armageddon, the last great war the world is going to fight. It will be fought in that same place where so many of the world's battles have been fought. From the beginning of time, Megiddo, Esdraelon, has been a bloody battlefield. At Megiddo the armies of the earth by the millions and the millions will converge to face that rendezvous with God. (According to Revelation 9:16 the armies of the east alone will number two hundred million men.) In the midst of this unimaginable holocaust, Christ intervenes in human history. He comes with his saints. "And I saw heaven opened, and behold a white horse; and he that sat upon him was called Faithful and True . . . his eyes were as a flame of fire, and on his head were many crowns

. . . And he was clothed with a vesture dipped in blood: and his name is called The Word of God. And the armies which were in heaven followed him upon white horses, clothed in fine linen, white and clean. And out of his mouth goeth a sharp sword, that with it he should smite the nations . . . and on his thigh a name written, KING OF KINGS, AND LORD OF LORDS" (Revelation 19:11–16). That is the intervention of God in human history. He delivers his people, shut up in the holy city, and he takes Satan and binds him for a thousand years in the bottomless pit.

What about the people who enter the millennium? The Scriptures reveal a two-fold judgment here. First, there is a judgment of the Gentiles (you have it translated "nations" in Matthew 25:32). All of those Gentiles who befriended God's preachers, his "brethren" who delivered God's message, will enter into the millennium. They received in faith the message and were kind to the messengers, their actions exemplifying their character. Then, according to Ezekiel, there will be a judgment of Israel (Ezekiel 20:33–38). Those that are at variance and refuse to receive their Messiah shall be cast out. Those that receive the Lord Jesus shall enter into the millennium, and for a thousand years they shall reign with Christ upon this earth, when the kingdom comes, and God's will is done in this weary world as it is in heaven.

At the end of the thousand years, Satan is released, one of the inexplicable revelations in prophecy. Satan is released, and some of those in the millennium who did not find their hearts in complete subservience to God, will rebel. There will be at that time the final conflict which ends forever man's rebellion against God.

78

We come now to the final resurrection of the wicked dead and the great white throne judgment. There the books are opened, and those whose names are not found written in the Lamb's Book of Life are cast out and rewarded according to their deeds. We (the Christians) are going to be rewarded when Jesus comes for us. They (the lost) are going to be rewarded at the great white throne judgment, according to their deeds. Death and the grave shall be cast into hell, into the fiery flames, and Satan shall be cast into that fury where the beast and the false prophet have already been for a thousand years.

Then will come the renovation. There will be a new heaven and a new earth, remade according to the fulness and the glory and the wonder of God. There will be a new heaven and a new earth, as it was in the beginning when God created the heavens and the earth. "And I John saw the holy city, new Jerusalem, coming down from God out of Heaven, prepared as a bride adorned for her husband. And I heard a great voice out of heaven saying, Behold, the tabernacle of God is with men, and he will dwell with them, and they shall be his people, and God himself shall be with them, and be their God" (as he intended in the beginning of the Garden of Eden, walking in the cool of the day). "And God shall wipe away all tears from their eyes; and there shall be no more death, neither sorrow, nor crying, neither shall there be any more pain: for the former things are passed away" (Revelation 21:2–4). No graves on the hillside of glory! No funeral wreaths on the doors of the mansions in the sky!

"And he that sat upon the throne said, Behold, I make all things new . . . I will give unto him that is athirst of the fountain of the water of life freely" (Revelation 23:5, 6). "And he shewed me a pure river of water of life, clear as crystal, proceeding out of the throne of God and of the Lamb . . . and on either side of the river, was there the tree of life" (from the Garden of Eden in the garden of God's paradise . . . "and the leaves of the tree were for the healing of the nations . . . And they shall see his face; and his name shall be in their foreheads . . . and they shall reign for ever and ever" (Revelation 1, 2, 4, 5).

"He which testifieth these things saith, Surely I come quickly. Amen. Even so, come, Lord Jesus" (Revelation 22:20). You know our hearts, we are ready. Anytime, Lord, any day, come. We are watching and waiting and praying. Come! God's atoning grace, The Scarlet Thread Through the Bible, has prepared our souls for glory. We are ready. Come!